# Living in an Ocean

Patty Whitehouse

Rourke

**Publishing LLC**

Vero Beach, Florida 32964

www.rourkepublishing.com

PHOTO CREDITS: © pufferfishy/dreamstime.com: page 18; © Dan Schmitt: title page; © Ablestock.com: page 4; © Paul Rogers: page 6; © Astrida Valigorsky: page 7; © Eliza Snow: page 8; © Jeffery Waibel: page 9; © PhotoDisc: pages 10, 19; © Renee Brady: page 11; © Digital Vision: pages 12, 13, 14, 15, 16; © Andrea Leone: page 17; © Dennis Sabo: page 20; © NOAA: page 21; © Dan Schmitt: page 22.

Editor: Robert Stengard-Olliges

Cover and interior design by Nicola Stratford

**Library of Congress Cataloging-in-Publication Data**

Whitehouse, Patricia, 1958-
  Living in an ocean / Patty Whitehouse.
      p. cm. --  (Animal habitats)
  Includes index.
  ISBN 1-60044-187-4 (hard cover)
  ISBN 1-59515-542-2 (soft cover)
  1.  Marine ecology--Juvenile literature. 2.  Ocean--Juvenile literature.  I. Title. II. Series: Whitehouse, Patricia, 1958- Animal habitats.
  QH541.5.S3W48 2007
  578.77--dc22
                                        2006017569

Printed in the USA

CG/CG

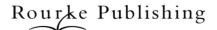

Rourke Publishing

www.rourkepublishing.com – sales@rourkepublishing.com
Post Office Box 3328, Vero Beach, FL 32964

# TABLE OF CONTENTS

# WHAT IS AN OCEAN?

Oceans are places with salty water. They cover most of the Earth. Some oceans are warm. Some are cold.

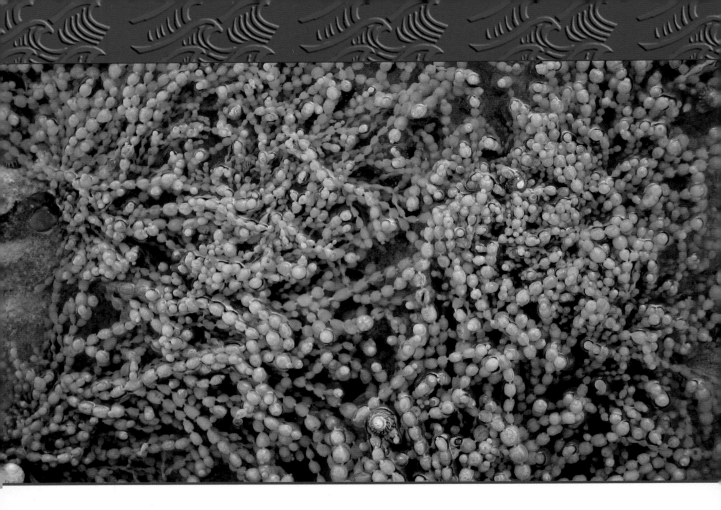

# HOW ARE OCEAN PLANTS DIFFERENT?

Most plants need a little water, but ocean plants live in water.

Some ocean plants are grasses. They grow in **shallow**, warm water.

# SEAWEEDS

Seaweed looks like a plant, but it does not have roots or stems. Scientists call seaweed **algae**.

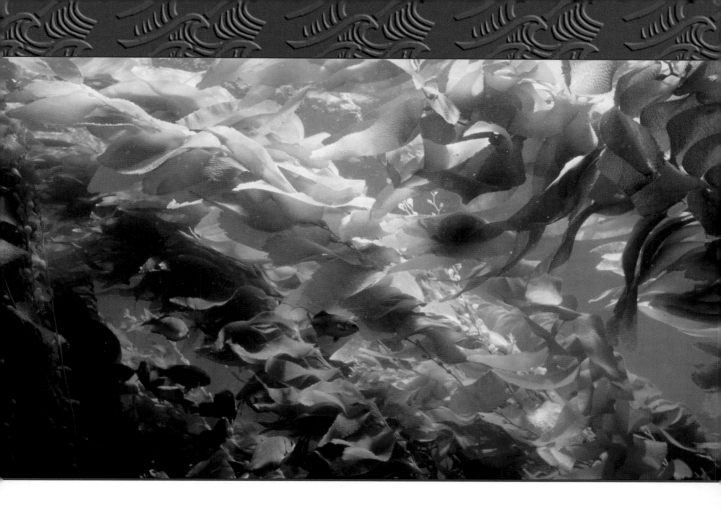

Seaweeds are red, green and brown. **Kelp** is seaweed that grows in beds.

# TiNY OCEAN ALGAE

Some algae are very small. They are called **phytoplankton**. Fish and whales eat them.

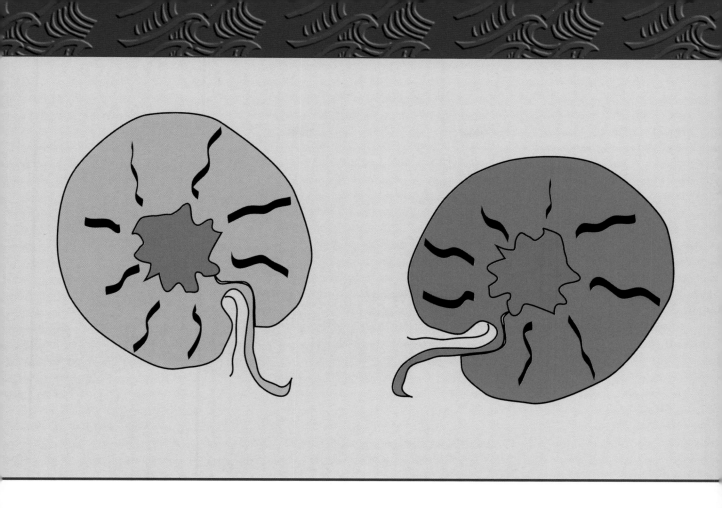

Some phytoplankton are round. Some are flat with tails. Some glow in the dark! Phytoplankton are too small to see with your eyes.

# HOW ARE OCEAN ANIMALS DIFFERENT?

Ocean animals can move in water. Fins, flippers or tails help them move.

Animals need **oxygen**. Some ocean animals get oxygen from water. Others, like dolphins hold their breath for a long time.

# CORAL REEFS

Corals are tiny animals. They live in the **reefs** they build.

Many animals live on coral reefs. Sponges, sea stars, and eels live there.

# FiNS aND FLippeRS

Sharks have fins. They help the shark move up, down, right, or left.

Penguins are birds that cannot fly. They have flippers that help them swim.

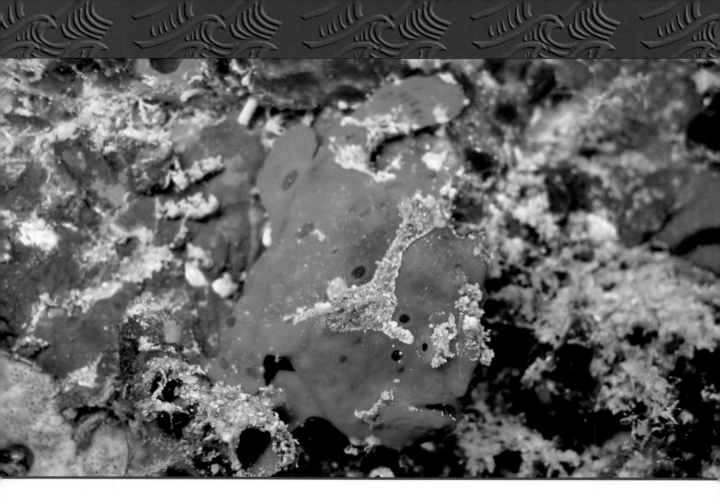

# Deep Sea Strangers

The anglerfish lives deep in the ocean where it is very dark. Part of its nose glows.

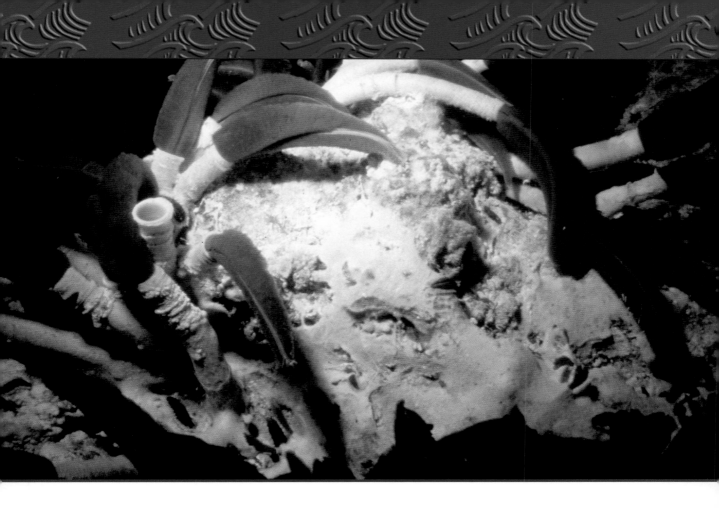

A tube worm lives on the dark ocean floor. They live in tubes. They grow as tall as a person.

# CAN PEOPLE LIVE IN OCEANS?

People can live near oceans, but they cannot stay in the ocean.

People can live in **submarines**. They can use
machines to learn about the ocean.

# GETTING AWAY

Some ocean animals eat squid, but squid fight back.
They squirt black ink. Then they swim away.

# Glossary

**algae** (AL gee) — plant-like living things without roots or stems

**kelp** (KELP) — seaweed that grows in beds

**oxygen** (OK suh juhn) — air or gas that animals breathe in

**phytoplankton** (FI toe plank TUN) — tiny ocean algae

**reef** (REEF) — hard structure corals build in the oceans

**shallow** (SHAL oh) — not very deep

**submarine** (SUHB muh reen) — boat that travels underwater

# Index

## FURTHER READING

Mara, Will. *The Four Oceans.* Children's Press, 2005.
O'Neill, Michael Patrick. *Let's Explore Coral Reefs*. Batfish Books, 2006.
Royston, Angela. *Oceans.* Heinemann, 2005.

## WEBSITES TO VISIT

www.mbgnet.net
www.enchantedlearning.com/coloring/oceanlife.shtml
www.yoto98.noaa.gov/kids.htm

## ABOUT THE AUTHOR

Patty Whitehouse has been a teacher for 17 years. She is currently a Lead Science teacher in Chicago, where she lives with her husband and two teenage children. She is the author of more than 100 books about science for children.

# ANIMAL HABITATS

This Discovery Library series explores six habitats and allows children to develop an appreciation for physical environments they may not yet know. Each book highlights some of the animals and plants that live and grow in a particular habitat. Each title in the series is focused on the NTSA standard for organisms and their environment. Designed for the early reader, the books feature images that enhance the text.

**Books In This Series Include:**

Living in a Desert: *covers plant and animal adaptations to dry climates*

Living in a Forest: *covers plant and animal adaptations to seasonal climates*

Living in a Grassland: *covers plant and animal adaptations to seasonal climates*

Living in a Rainforest: *covers plant and animal adaptations to wet climates*

Living in an Ocean: *covers plant and animal adaptations to ocean environments*

Living in the Arctic: *covers plant and animal adaptations to cold climates*

ISBN 1-59515-542-2

9 781595 155429

90000

Rourke Publishing